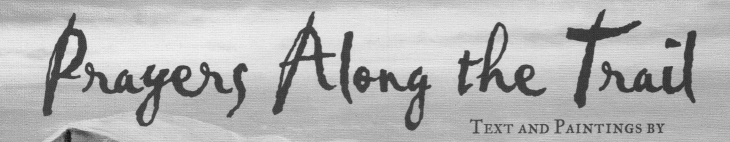

Prayers Along the Trail

Text and Paintings by

Jack Terry

HARVEST HOUSE PUBLISHERS

EUGENE, OREGON

Prayers Along the Trail

Text Copyright © 2003 by Jack Terry
Published by Harvest House Publishers
Eugene, Oregon 97402

Library of Congress Cataloging-in-Publication Data
Terry, Jack, 1952-
    Prayers along the trail / Jack Terry.
        p. cm.
    ISBN 0-7369-1025-5
    1. Cowboys--Religious life. I. Title.
    BV4596.C65 T475 2003
    242--dc21
        2002011141

Design and production by Koechel Peterson & Associates, Inc., Minneapolis, Minnesota

Unless otherwise indicated, Scripture quotations are from the New American Standard Bible®,
© 1960, 1962, 1971, 1972, 1973, 1975, 1977 by The Lockman Foundation. Used by permission.
Scripture quotations marked NIV are taken from the Holy Bible, New International Version®,
Copyright © 1973, 1978, 1984 by the International Bible Society. Used by permission of Zondervan
Publishing House.

Harvest House Publishers has made every effort to trace the ownership of all poems and quotes.
In the event of a question arising from the use of a poem or quote, we regret any error made and
will be pleased to make the necessary correction in future editions of this book.

Printed in Hong Kong

03 04 05 06 07 08 09 10 / NG / 10 9 8 7 6 5 4 3 2

CONTENTS

Preface

So many books have been written on the subject of prayer throughout the years because it is such a tremendous blessing to be able to communicate directly with the Creator of all things. This great privilege belongs to everyone who invites Jesus Christ to come live within their heart. God has provided a way of salvation through the sacrifice of His Son for everyone who will believe.

I hope you will enjoy this brief examination of the prayer that Jesus shared with His disciples. I have written a poem referring to "The Lord's Prayer" from a cowboy's perspective and one I identify with whole-heartedly. I urge you to focus on the majesty of your Father in heaven and be thankful for His unequaled grace and love in your life.

DEDICATION

To everyone, everywhere, who supports the right to pray.

"The Cowboy's Prayer"

Dear Lord, God in heaven, from my bedroll on the ground—
I can't help but see Your majesty in the stars sparkling all around.
Your Good Book says You have a name for every star I see above,
I know You're looking at me too, for I can feel Your love.

Now some people dress in fancy clothes and call upon the Lord,
And some folks fill a pew up front, but sleep because they're bored.
I prefer to talk to You astride a sure enough good, stout steed.
Ridin' across a prairie, Lord, Your company is all I need.

Lord, I thank You that You've put me here with a job I love to do;
Never was much on schoolin', thought I'd leave the thinking mostly up to You.
You've taught me right from wrong and how to work upon this land.
You've fed my family, warmed our home, and made our lives so grand.

Lord, let me work honest and strong for the wages I draw today
There's so much more to life than what I bring home in my pay.
I know there will be food on our table, we've never gone hungry yet;
You've been the provider of all our needs from the very first day we met.

Forgive me, Lord, when I do the things I know I should not do,
And if I hurt a man with what I say, remind me those words were not from You.
Please search the thoughts I never speak and also search my heart,
Make me as clean as clean can be, just like I was at the very start.

Many a man has done me wrong, few times have I been treated fair.
I know You said forgive them all and dear God, make this my prayer.
But Lord, it's so hard to forget every hurt that I've got stored up inside,
By Your power and love, I forgive them right now, and bury my own selfish pride.

Lord, keep me safe on this trail I ride, and if sometimes I drift from Your plan,
Guide me back gently to the land that I love, with the touch of Your awesome big hand.
The stars up above, I know You named every one, and I see my name written there,
One day I'll ride home, peace and joy for my own, with not one single worry or care.

Introduction

While the American cowboy may not be the most educated and eloquent individual in our society, I hope you will appreciate some valuable insight on prayer from his point of view. Prayer has been, from the beginning of time, the principal means by which men and women, created in the image of God, have expressed their dependence on Him for everything. No one has ever understood this better than the American cowboy. Daniel Webster described prayer as "an approach to deity in word or thought, an earnest request, the act of praying to God." A cowboy, in his typically simplistic manner, would probably just say, "Prayer is talking and listening to God."

When I can't ride anymore, I shall still keep horses as long as I can hobble about with a bucket and a wheelbarrow. When I can't hobble, I shall roll my wheelchair out to the fence of the field where my horses graze, and watch them.

MONICA DICKENS

Our Father in Heaven

Our Father who art in heaven, Hallowed be Thy name (Matthew 6:9).

DEAR LORD, GOD IN HEAVEN, FROM MY BEDROLL ON THE GROUND—
I CAN'T HELP BUT SEE YOUR MAJESTY IN THE STARS SPARKLING ALL AROUND.
YOUR GOOD BOOK SAYS YOU HAVE A NAME FOR EVERY STAR I SEE ABOVE,
I KNOW YOU'RE LOOKING AT ME TOO, FOR I CAN FEEL YOUR LOVE.

Cowboys at the turn of the century had a very special feeling about God and still do. They understood the vastness of nature and the elements which they faced daily, and the importance of spending time alone in the presence of the Almighty. If it didn't rain, their livestock suffered. If it rained too much, it meant several days in a wet saddle trying to save their livelihood from perilous waters. As they climbed in their musty canvas bedrolls at night and gazed at millions of stars above, they had no problem realizing their smallness in the Lord's great creation and their total dependence upon His guiding hand.

The long and often dangerous cattle trails didn't leave a cowboy much time for being with his family or much less attending church. His bedroll was often the loneliest of places, filled with the memories of everything he left behind to pursue his dream of riding the open range and punching cattle. On many nights he gazed into the galaxy flat on his back. As he peered into infinity, he could almost smell his mother's hot apple pie and the scent of his dad's smokehouse. How he longed to be home, enjoying a Sunday afternoon picnic under the big shade tree in their backyard.

My granddad shared many stories with me about his life as a cowboy. While everything within his being wanted to be a real-life, full-grown cowboy, he was only seventeen when he left home and he sure did miss his family. He said he could never forget his mama's tears as he rode away to join his first cattle drive. His daddy just turned his back and walked toward the barn like he had something really important to tend to, reaching up to rub something from his eyes.

Granddad thought of his family every night while he was on the trail. He wondered if his little sister was sitting by the upstairs window, braiding her hair by the lantern light just like Mama had taught her. He was almost certain his little brother was listening as Grandpa Williams softly picked "Amazing Grace" from his rocker on the front porch just before bedtime.

Just prior to dozing off to sleep, Granddad was startled from his dreams when a hawk screeched from the night sky above. His eyes were filled with a million blinking stars as the promise he made to his mother before he left home echoed in his mind: He would never let a night go by without saying his prayers and this night would be no exception.

He began to softly utter the prayer his mother had taught him as a boy, "Our Father who art in heaven," was all he could manage to say. The young cowboy became overwhelmed by the magnitude of the universe above him. As his eyes searched the sky from left to right as far as he could see, he began to wonder, "How big must God be to create all this?" While he lay there flat on his back he remembered a Bible story my great grandmother had told him on a very similar night a long, long time ago. He thought it was from Isaiah, in the Old Testament, somewhere around chapter forty.

Lying there staring at the stars, curiosity finally got the best of him. As Cookie and the rest of the cowboys were snoring beneath their canvas bags, he borrowed a lantern from the chuckwagon, pulled a dry match from the chuck drawer, and soon had enough light to locate his grandpa's tattered old Bible in his saddle bags. Fumbling through the dog-eared, onionskin pages in the dim light, he finally found Isaiah. The story was all coming back to him. He recalled how his grandmother always loved the little baby lambs that were born every spring on their ranch. But being a real cowboy, Granddad naturally preferred cows to sheep any day. Sheep cried too much and weren't very smart. He said they were so dumb they would follow each other right over the edge of a cliff until all were hopelessly lost.

Reading on, he realized that God tends His flock like a shepherd. He gathers the lambs in His arms and carries them close to His heart, gently leading those that have young. The same God that made all the stars in the sky loves even the smallest, dumbest, and smelliest of creatures.

It is not enough for a man to learn how to ride; he must learn how to fall.

MEXICAN PROVERB

As he read verse 12, "Who has measured the waters in the hollow of His hand," suddenly he realized that God is big, really big. He began to think about the words of Isaiah describing how God can hold all the waters on the earth in the hollow of His hand. What the prophet Isaiah and the cowboy didn't know then, that we know now, is how much water there is on our planet. There are five major oceans in our world. The Atlantic Ocean alone is said to measure about 33,420,000 square miles and hold 85 million cubic miles of water. A cubic mile measures one mile wide, by one mile deep, by one mile high, and equals more than one trillion gallons. The Pacific Ocean is comprised of some 141 million cubic miles of water. All the water on the earth measures some 326 million cubic miles of water according to modern scientists.

The second half of verse 12 reads "or with the breadth of his hands marked off the heavens" (NIV). As Granddad held his hand up toward the night sky, he was amazed by the immensity of the

I took to the life of a cowboy like a horse takes to oats.
CLINTON McCOY

galaxy. He told me that as many nights as he had spent outside, he had never noticed how many stars there were in the sky. We now have a lot more scientifically proven information than the young cowboy or Isaiah did.

Modern technology tells us that our earth is some 25,000 miles in circumference and 8,000 miles in diameter. However, earth is only a part of the small galaxy we know as the Milky Way containing billons of stars. If we were to travel from one side of the Milky Way to the other at the speed of light (186,000 miles per second) it would take 100,000 years. There are 20 galaxies in our corner of the universe. It would take 2.5 million years to travel through those galaxies at the speed of light. Many scientists believe there are more than 1 billion galaxies, each with 100 billion stars. Psalm 147:4,5 reads, "He counts the number of the stars; He gives names to all of them. Great is our Lord, and abundant in strength; His understanding is infinite." Just as sure as it was difficult for my granddad to understand the magnitude of God, we, too, should stand in awe of His limitless wisdom and power.

While we may not be able to totally grasp the complexity of God, we can identify with the reality of His love. The God who chose to create everything and named every star in the universe did so simply because He is love. Every person was created in the image of God and has the ability to reflect His character. Jesus said we should address God as "Our Father in heaven." Mere words cannot express what a privilege it is to be part of the family of God and to talk personally with the Creator of the universe as one of His children.

While God is both holy and majestic, He is also loving and personally interested in His family. The apostle Paul describes God in Acts 17:24-28 (NIV): "The God who made the world and everything in it is the Lord of heaven and earth... From one man he made every nation of men, that they should inhabit the whole earth; and he determined the times set for them and the exact places where they should live. For in him we live and move and have our being..."

If my granddad were here today, he would simply tell you from experience that the God who created all things—every single star in the sky, every drop of water in every ocean, every cute little lamb, and every cowboy who ever saddled a horse, desires that no person should perish, but all would come to know Him as their "Father who art in heaven."

IN THE STEADY GAZE OF THE HORSE SHINES A SILENT ELOQUENCE
THAT SPEAKS OF LOVE, LOYALTY, STRENGTH AND COURAGE.
IT IS THE WINDOW THAT REVEALS TO US HOW WILLING IS HIS SPIRIT,
HOW GENEROUS HIS HEART.

L. McGuire

God's Kingdom and Will

Thy kingdom come. Thy will be done, on earth as it is in heaven (Matthew 6:10).

LORD, I THANK YOU THAT YOU'VE PUT ME HERE WITH A JOB I LOVE TO DO;
NEVER WAS MUCH ON SCHOOLIN', THOUGHT I'D LEAVE THE THINKING MOSTLY UP TO YOU.
YOU'VE TAUGHT ME RIGHT FROM WRONG AND HOW TO WORK UPON THIS LAND.
YOU'VE FED MY FAMILY, WARMED OUR HOME, AND MADE OUR LIVES SO GRAND.

God's kingdom today is present in the hearts of everyone whom He calls His children. When we pray that God's will be done, we pray that His perfect purpose will be accomplished in this world and throughout eternity. As a child of God, we know that He loves and cares for us personally. He wants us to see His will fulfilled in our lives.

I like what John Wayne once said, "There's right and there's wrong. You get to do one or the other. You do one and you're living. You do the other and you may be walking around but you're as dead as a beaver hat." Now that's a little cowboy logic that's easy to understand. When we choose to walk outside the boundaries God has ordained in our lives, we usually suffer disappointment. When we are not in His perfect will, we are not able to successfully contribute to His kingdom here on earth.

About 25 years ago, I had an opportunity to do something right, as John Wayne put it, and in doing so, I was incredibly blessed. I was a young aspiring western artist making a so-called living as a part-time cowboy, raising a couple of horses and a few cows, and day-working whenever I could for a few extra bucks to buy art supplies. It was Christmas Eve and my family and I were going through some rather difficult financial

times. The afternoon mail brought me a Christmas card from my parents with a crisp $100 bill neatly tucked inside. What marvelous timing since I didn't have enough money to buy many presents for our family! It was getting late and the stores would be closing early, so I quickly headed my pickup toward town.

It was very cold that December afternoon and the wind was blowing hard out of the north. A light dusting of snow still covered the ground from the night before. Just before I made the turn off our road toward town, I passed the small wood frame ranch house that was surrounded by brush and scrubby trees. It sat back off the farm-to-market road about 100 yards and was hard to see unless you were really looking for it. I had briefly met the cowhand and his family who lived there several months back, and I often waved at the children playing outside in the yard when I drove by.

As I sped past the house, I saw two little girls and a boy playing in the front yard. At that moment, I felt an overwhelming sense that God wanted me to stop. I didn't want to stop. I had important Christmas shopping to do, so I drove on about a mile down the road. But the feeling intensified, so I turned around and went back to the house, sensing that God had something more important to accomplish.

When I got out of the car, the entire family came over to greet me. One little girl asked me if I wanted to see their Christmas decorations. I said yes, and she took me by the hand and we all went inside the dilapidated old farmhouse. It was adorned for the season in an array of construction paper decorations and strings of popcorn hung from the cedar tree they cut from their pasture. While it was a very heart-warming experience, I couldn't help but notice it was freezing cold in the house. They had no fireplace and did not have enough money to replace the old woodstove that rusted out last year. All the water in the house was frozen and

Good judgment comes from experience, and a lot of that comes from bad judgment.

COWBOY WISDOM

everyone was bundled in coats and blankets day and night trying to stay warm. The five children ranged in age from two years to seven and I was concerned for their safety.

As I drove away, the entire family stood on the front porch and waved. I knew I had heard from God but thought if I hurried, I might find them a little electric heater that would give them enough heat for the night and still have enough time and money left to do some Christmas shopping. It was now almost 4:00 P.M. and most of the stores in town would be closed on Christmas Eve. As I was heading to the mall on the other side of town, I passed a flea market. Standing in the middle of the parking lot in front of the store was a big black woodstove with a sign on it that read $100. The writing was on the wall. You can probably surmise what happened next.

A cowboy is a man with guts and a horse.
WILL JAMES

The children's father and I had the new stove installed just before dark and with enough wood from our house to last through the holidays. They were so thankful for a warm Christmas. One of the young girls said it was the best Christmas they ever had. It was certainly one of the best for me.

The very next morning around 8:00 A.M. we heard a knock at our front door. I gazed out the window surprised to see my Sunday School teacher, Ray Lewis, standing on the front porch. As I opened the door, he said, "Merry Christmas" and handed me an envelope. Inside was a check for almost $150. He said our class had taken up a collection and wanted us to have it. I learned that day how God's kingdom is alive in the hearts of His people and how God uses people just like you and me to carry out His perfect will.

Like John Wayne said, it is good to do the right thing.

A man on a horse is spiritually, as well as physically, bigger than a man on foot.
JOHN STEINBECK

Daily Bread

Give us this day our daily bread (Matthew 6:11).

Lord, let me work honest and strong for the wages I draw today
There's so much more to life than what I bring home in my pay.
I know there will be food on our table, we've never gone hungry yet;
You've been the provider of all our needs from the very first day we met.

God is the provider of everything we need. It is through His great love for us that He sustains us daily. "Our daily bread" refers to everything necessary to sustain our lives. I believe it not only applies to our physical lives but our spiritual lives as well. Jesus refers to Himself as "the bread of life" in John 6:35 and it is through our sacramental communion with the bread that we are reminded of His great sacrifice on the cross of Calvary. I am not proud to admit that there have been times in my life when I have actually taken pride in the fact that I was self-made, strong, and independent and didn't need any help from anyone. Because I was focused on myself and not on the holiness and majesty of God, I failed to realize that everything I have and all that I am is a result of His perfect provision.

There have been so many times in my life where I can look back and see how God provided exactly what I needed, when I needed it. Sometimes God even gave me far more than what I needed. One such time was during the energy crisis in the 1980s and very few people were buying western art. I really needed some customers since most of the oil money in Texas had dried up. I had to sell some art quick or get a real job. My wife decided I should think about going

back to work on a ranch since I loved the life of a cowboy so much. The money wasn't that great but at least the work was steady.

It was a big weekend in town as we were hosting the Texas State Arts & Crafts Fair. Thousands of tourists came from all over Texas and neighboring states to visit the three-day event. A local gallery owner rented a big red and white tent, tied balloons and banners all over it, spread hay bales throughout, and hung 29 of my paintings. We were set up on the busiest street corner in town. Believe me, everybody saw us. I must admit I felt more like a circus clown than a cowboy artist, but I was desperate.

Friday night came and we had a lot of lookers, but no one bought anything. Most everyone who came were locals making circus jokes at our expense. We showed up bright and early Saturday morning, confidently dressed in our finest western apparel and ready to put a painting in the trunk of the first 29 cars that showed up. You see, a truly seasoned artist must be an eternal optimist. Once again, we had a lot of lookers, but no takers. Not even one measly offer. By mid-afternoon Saturday, I have to admit, my confidence was waning when some friends from church stopped by to lend moral support. They had been praying for months for our business to improve and this day they prayed for new customers to come to the show and buy every single painting we had. I must confess my faith was weak. I thought, as they prayed, how happy I would be to just sell one.

Right before we were ready to load up late that afternoon, not one sale for the entire weekend, a man and his wife strolled into the tent. They were in town from Iowa and said they wanted to buy some authentic western art. After about a half hour of looking

The most beautiful, the most spirited and the most inspiring creature ever to print foot on the grasses of America.

J. FRANK DOBIE

at and discussing the art, the man said "If I buy them all, will you deliver them to Des Moines?" I'm sure you can guess my answer. Despite my lack of faith that afternoon, God provided so much more than my daily bread. What had begun as an embarrassment for a young artist in need of encouragement, ended up a blessing and was a significant turning point in my professional career.

Our daily bread is the very sustenance we need to fulfill God's will for our entire life here on earth. All we have to do is put our faith in Him. He will provide. He always has and He always will.

The sunshine's golden gleam is thrown,
On sorrel, chestnut, bay, and roan.
OLIVER WENDELL HOLMES

WITHOUT THE HORSE WHAT WOULD HAVE BECOME OF MAN?
IT HAS SERVED US FOR TRANSPORT, IN AGRICULTURE, INDUSTRY,
AND EVERY KIND OF ACTIVITY SINCE THE DAWN OF TIME.

BERTRAND LECLAIR

Forgive Us as We Forgive

Forgive us our debts, as we also have forgiven our debtors (Matthew 6:12).

Forgive me, Lord, when I do the things I know I should not do,
And if I hurt a man with what I say, remind me those words were not from You.
Please search the thoughts I never speak and also search my heart,
Make me as clean as clean can be, just like I was at the very start.

Many a man has done me wrong, few times have I been treated fair.
I know You said forgive them all and dear God, make this my prayer.
But Lord, it's so hard to forget every hurt that I've got stored up inside,
By Your power and love, I forgive them right now, and bury my own selfish pride.

Forgiveness is a top priority with God. Jesus mentions the importance of forgiveness in His model prayer in Matthew 12 but then uses verses 14 and 15 to emphasize the necessity of total forgiveness. "For if you forgive men for their transgressions, your heavenly Father will also forgive you. But if you do not forgive men, then your Father will not forgive your transgressions."

Can you imagine the God who named every star and holds all the water on our planet in the cup of His hands not forgiving you? When we do not forgive others as God has forgiven us, we deny that we are sinners in need of His forgiveness.

In God's eyes, we are all alike. He created each individual in His image that we might be reflections of His glory. He loves every single thing that He created and

"The Lord is not slow in keeping his promise, as some understand slowness. He is patient with you, not wanting anyone to
perish but everyone to come to repentance" (2 Peter 3:9 NIV).

For most of us, it is easy to ask God for forgiveness but it's
hard for us to forgive others. Jesus told a parable of the unforgiving
debtor in Matthew 18:21–35. Peter asked Jesus , "Lord, how many
times shall I forgive my brother when he sins against me?
Up to seven times?"

When Peter asked Jesus about forgiveness, he
knew that the rabbis taught it was necessary to forgive
people three times if they offend you. In his attempt
to be generous, Peter asked if seven times was enough. Jesus
said that we should forgive people who truly repent every
time they ask—the very same way God forgives us. If
we choose not to forgive, we separate ourselves from
the fellowship of God's love. The choice is ours to make.

An old-time cowboy in west Texas told me a story of a cattle drive he rode on when he was a young man. Bill had worked for several years alongside six other cowboys for Mr. Buddy Johnson on a large ranch known as the Bar 7. Even though Bill was very young, Mr. Johnson chose him to be the trail boss from Texas to Kansas, causing some jealousy among the other cowboys. Bill had proven himself to be a good, dependable cowboy and he was as honest as they came. Mr. Johnson had quite a reputation as a good judge of character from his service in the Civil War and knew Bill was the best man in his outfit.

Mr. Johnson ran about 700 head on the Bar 7 and he wanted to get them to market before winter set in up north. He rode with the cowboys every mile of the way to keep an eye on his sizeable investment. He dispatched Bill out ahead of the herd to scout a good place to make camp near water and to be on the guard for any rustlers or unfriendly Indians. Bill often had to ride two or more days out and then back again before he found a suitable spot to rest the cattle.

It was necessary not to move the herd too fast in the heat because they would lose too much weight. The stockyards paid for the cattle by the pound so great care was taken not to push them too fast and to make sure they had plenty to eat and drink. Bill performed his duties flawlessly and with great pride. The cattle were moved an average of ten miles a day and almost every night they camped by water. The cows always seemed to be calmer near the water and rested better through the night.

While the cows were moving calmly along and the weather was being cooperative, some of the other cowboys were becoming increasingly jealous of Bill. Mr. Johnson paid them little attention and they felt like they were doing all the work while Bill rode out leisurely in search of new campsites. While they were ridin' drag,

This most noble beast is the most beautiful, the swiftest, and of the highest courage of domesticated animals.
PEDRO GARCIA CONDE

and eatin' dust during the day and beans at night, they wrongly speculated that Bill was living it up in town somewhere. They spent their evenings scheming up ways to get rid of Bill. If they could cut Bill out of his share, it meant more money for all of them come payday.

Bill had set up camp that night along the banks of a river. The chuckwagon fire was growing dim and all but the night-herding cowboys were in their bedrolls. Suddenly, a loud crash of lightning dropped from the northern sky above. It was the first cold front of the year and it was a big one. Thunder and lightning crashed all around. Every single cowboy jumped from his bedroll and headed for his horse. This was stampede weather!

All at once, the cattle were aroused from their sleep and up on their feet, nervously moving about. Bill was the first cowboy to be horseback and tried to make his way to the cattle closest to the river. He knew if there was a stampede, he had to turn them away from the water or many would drown. But before he could reach

I love the horse from hoof to head.
JAMES WHITCOMB RILEY

the lead steer, another bolt of lightning crashed to the ground and the cattle bolted. Bill rode headlong into the river. He thought if he crossed before the cattle, he could turn the leader back leaving the other cowboys in position to head them off and eventually calm them down. Bill's horse, Old Dan, was a good swimmer and he was sure he would beat the cows to the other side. By that time, most of the cowboys were horseback but could do nothing to stop the herd. They were too late, and Mr. Johnson yelled for them to stay away from the river.

Suddenly Old Dan dropped about a foot and could not keep his head above water. It was quicksand and there was nothing Bill could do in the fast current unless someone threw him a rope. Frantically looking over his shoulder toward camp, he could see three cowboys. He yelled for a rope but no one reached for his lariat. *Maybe they couldn't hear him,* he thought. But then from behind the cowboys rode Mr. Johnson, swinging his rope above the heads of the stampeding cattle. Bill managed to catch it and

dallied it around the saddle horn. With Old Dan fighting to get out of the sand and struggling desperately to breathe, he signaled his boss and yelled, "Pull!"

Old Dan was too tired to fight any longer and Bill had to make a decision. He could tie the rope around himself and be pulled to safety or jump off and hopefully reduce the burden enough so the horse could break free and be pulled ashore. By this time, all the cowboys were watching as Bill leapt from his saddle into the raging river and disappeared into the darkness. Mr. Johnson's horse finally managed to pull Old Dan free and soon everyone was searching for Bill.

Most of the storm front had blown through and the lightning had subsided when one of the cowboys found Bill several hundred yards down river where he had finally managed to swim to shore. He was exhausted but his first question was about his horse. "Did you save him?" The cowboy just nodded as they made their way back to camp.

Cookie had the fire started by the time they returned and everyone gathered 'round. The cattle had all disappeared into the night and would soon have to be recovered. But Mr. Johnson sternly asked all the cowboys why they didn't help Bill. Every wet Stetson pointed toward the ground, no one uttered a single word. Just then a tired, wet, skinny young cowboy stood up and said, "Don't worry fellers, I probably would have done the same thing if I were in your boots. How about we saddle up and go get them cows."

It took a lot of courage for Bill to say that. Let's look beyond the young cowboy's simplicity and analyze what he really said. "I forgive each one of you cowboys. I know you did me wrong, but I probably would've done the same thing if I were in your boots. Now we have a job to do and it takes every single one of us to do it, so saddle up, let's ride."

Bill knew unless he completely forgave them, they would never be able to work together and get the cattle to market on time. He also understood the jealousy the other cowboys had for him. He had felt the same way just a few short years ago. Youthful ambition sometimes blinds our vision from the truth.

We have a choice just like Bill did. Do we sink or swim? We can choose to forgive and be forgiven or not forgive and be separated from the fellowship of God's love.

Their horses were of great stature, strong and clean-limbed; their grey coats glistened, their long tails flowed in the wind, their manes were braided on their proud necks.

J.R.R. TOLKIEN

THE PIONEERS AND RANCHERS OF THE FRONTIER WOULD NEVER HAVE MADE
THE WEST HABITABLE HAD IT NOT BEEN FOR THESE WILD COWBOYS,
THESE...HARD-RIDING, HARD-LIVING RANGERS OF THE BARRENS,
THESE EASY, COOL, LACONIC, SIMPLE YOUNG MEN WHOSE BLOOD WAS TINGED
WITH FIRE AND WHO POSSESSED A MAGNIFICENT AND TERRIBLE
EFFRONTERY TOWARD DANGER AND DEATH.

Zane Grey
The Man of the Forest

Protect Us from Evil

And do not lead us into temptation, but deliver us from evil (Matthew 6:13).

LORD, KEEP ME SAFE ON THIS TRAIL THAT I RIDE, AND IF SOMETIMES I DRIFT FROM YOUR PLAN,
GUIDE ME BACK GENTLY TO THE LAND THAT I LOVE, WITH THE TOUCH OF YOUR AWESOME BIG HAND.
THE STARS UP ABOVE, I KNOW YOU NAMED EVERY ONE, AND I SEE MY NAME WRITTEN THERE,
ONE DAY I'LL RIDE HOME, PEACE AND JOY FOR MY OWN, WITH NOT ONE SINGLE WORRY OR CARE.

While God does not lead us into temptation, He sometimes allows those whom He loves to be tested. My dad always says it builds character. Even Jesus was tempted by Satan just as we are today. All of us struggle with temptations of one sort or another but God said in 1 Corinthians 10:13 (NIV), "No temptation has seized you except what is common to man. And God is faithful: he will not let you be tempted beyond what you can bear. But when you are tempted, he will also provide a way out so that you can stand up under it."

This brings to mind a fine old cowboy gentleman from New Mexico. He wrangled on some of the best ranches in New Mexico and Arizona all of his life. Jim Wescott was forced to hang up his spurs a few years ago because the strenuous life as a working cowboy had finally taken its toll. After many broken bones, bruises, and near death experiences, he now sits and reminisces of days gone by.

Jim shares how jobs were scarce for cowboys because ranch owners had a very difficult time making ends meet through droughts, depressions, and diseases. A young cowboy who had not yet gained a reputation in the saddle often had to prove himself before he could sign on

permanently. Money was too hard to come by to waste on a cowboy who wasn't worth his salt. If he was lucky enough to be hired, 1946 wages were $90 a month plus a cot in the bunkhouse and three meals a day. Jim recalls how he was put to the test on his first job on the Panama Ranch in the Guadalupe Mountains of New Mexico.

Ranch owners and foremen were not always sure of the new cowboys. They wanted to test their abilities with a rope and in the saddle. Often times they paired the new cowboy with the rankest horse in the outfit—the one that nobody wanted to ride. Jim recalls how the owner told him, "If you can ride the night horse in the morning, you can work for the Panama." Jim could hardly wait until morning. This young cowboy was sure there had never been a horse he couldn't ride. "Getting this job would be a cinch," he thought.

The night horse was the horse they kept in the corral and was used to wrangle the other horses from the pasture before work began that day. The wrangler's job was to rise from his bunk long before daylight, saddle the night horse, and gather the rest of the remuda before breakfast. The horses were penned just before sun up in the corral, waiting to be saddled for the day's work.

It seems the Panama had about a dozen horses that had not yet been saddle-broke. The boss had fired the last wrangler and none of the other cowboys in the outfit had the ability nor the inclination to break the horses. There was one horse in the bunch that was particularly mean-spirited and no one was ever able to ride him. The owner had named him Satan. He thought it would be interesting to switch him with the night horse to see how young Jim could handle him in the morning. He would put the young cowboy to the test to find out if he had the makings of a wrangler or not.

Jim turned in early that night after supper. Most of the other cowboys didn't have much to say to him anyway. They seldom welcomed a stranger until he had proven himself to be a good

His life was the life of a cowboy. He realized his former vision of himself, booted, sombreroed, and revolvered, passing his days in the saddle.

FRANK NORRIS — *McTeague*

hand. He crawled out of his bedroll long before daylight. He threw his saddle over one shoulder carrying his blanket and bridle in the other hand as his spurs jingled through the darkness toward the corral where he thought the night horse awaited.

By the time he had walked the 50-some odd yards to the corral, he happened to notice a light on in the main ranch house. He could see the owner silhouetted in front of the window on the veranda and several of the other cowboys nearby. This was very unusual he thought, since most of them would normally sleep for another 30 minutes to an hour. Nevertheless, he had a job to do and he opened the corral gate and went about his business.

He had no longer latched the gate behind him before the big brown horse reared up on his hind legs and began coming at him, pawing with his front legs. At that moment, Jim figured he had been set up. He had two choices. He could either quit and move on to another ranch or prove himself and fight for the job he wanted. He could hear the other cowboys chuckling from the veranda. He was tempted to gather his things and ride off. But in a split second, he grabbed his lariat rope and caught Satan around the neck. After a dust-filled fight around the corral, he choked him down and slipped the bridle over his head.

Satan stood up and Jim threw his blanket and saddle over his back with one hand, keeping a tight hold on the reins with the other. With one foot in the stirrup he flung himself up on Satan's back and the rodeo began. After about 10 or 12 seconds of bucking, jumping, twisting, and snorting, Jim said "Satan throwed me higher than the saddle house roof." But that ride was 10 or 12 seconds longer than anyone else had ever stayed on Satan's back and the cowboys cheered as Jim scraped himself off the corral floor and gathered his tack.

It's a lot like nuts and bolts—if the rider's nuts, the horse bolts!

Nicholas Evans

It was now time for breakfast and the boss came over to the corral and offered Jim his hand. "Son, my wife's fixin' steak, gravy, and biscuits with syrup. Come on over to the house and let's have some breakfast. The horses won't mind waiting awhile."

Jim made quite an impression on the boss and the other cowboys. He had his first real paying job as a cowboy. He soon received an additional $25 a month for breaking horses. He not only passed the test but his life became an example to the other cowboys on the ranch.

Many times in life we are faced with trials and temptations just like Jim was. Sometimes we are deceived and sometimes we are simply weak. We are all human and we all make mistakes but our Father in heaven has lovingly provided a way out for us.

As we pray for God to deliver us from evil, it is essential to remember that the provisions He has already made on our behalf ensure our victory as we appropriate them. It is our responsibility to pray, to resist temptation, and finally, to fight the spiritual forces which seek to destroy us. Just as young Jim had his chaps, boots, bridle, bit, rope, and hat to ride "Satan," we too are promised in the Bible of our protective armor God has provided for us to do battle (see Ephesians 6).

Timothy's advice is for us to flee anything we consider to be a temptation (2 Timothy 2:22). Sometimes we must stand up and fight for what is right. As we pursue and model the qualities of holiness that God had reserved for His children, we may be responsible for the salvation of others. We can learn a lot from the life of cowboy Jim Wescott. He was tempted, but he resisted and fought back with all his might. He was rewarded for his actions and to paraphrase Timothy, the other cowboys who opposed him came to their senses.

No hour of life is wasted that is spent in the saddle.

WINSTON CHURCHILL